W9-BYC-122

FOLK

SOUNDS OF MUSIC

David and Patricia Armentrout

The Rourke Corporation, Inc.
Vero Beach, Florida 32964

PHOTO CREDITS:
© Oscar C. Williams: cover, title page, page 17; © Sue Anderson: page 4;
© Archive Photos: page 7; © Bruce Carr: page 8; © Kim Karpeles: pages 10, 13, 21; © Kay L. Hendrich: page 12; © Reuters/Lee Celano/Archive Photos: page 15; © Armentrout: page 18

PRODUCED BY:
East Coast Studios, Merritt Island, Florida

CREATIVE SERVICES:
Susan Albury

Library of Congress Cataloging-in-Publication Data

Armentrout, David. 1962-
    Folk / by David and Patricia Armentrout.
        p. cm. — (Sounds of music)
    Includes bibliographical references (p. 24) and index.
    Summary: Discusses the popularity of traditional folk music, its styles, and musical instruments.
    ISBN 0-86593-532-7
    1. Folk music—History and criticism Juvenile literature. [1. Folk music.]
I. Armentrout, Patricia, 1960- II. Title. III. Series
ML3928.A77 1999
781.62—dc21   99-20059
                                                                          CIP

Printed in the USA

TABLE OF CONTENTS

What Is Music?   5
Folk Music   6
Spreading the News   9
The Ballad   11
The Epic   14
Work Songs   16
Folk Music Changes   19
Instruments   20
Popular Folk Tunes   22
Glossary   23
Index   24
Further Reading   24

WHAT IS MUSIC?

Can you explain what music is? Is music the sound of voices singing? Is music the sound of instruments playing? When did music begin?

No one really knows how and when music began. Music may have started with the pounding of a drum. The first music may have been a mother humming softly to her child. Maybe the first music was a story sung with a pretty tune.

Interest in music can begin at an early age.

FOLK MUSIC

Folk music is an old music style. Folk music has a **tradition** (truh DISH en). Tradition is the passing down of beliefs or stories by showing or telling. These beliefs are continued and become "traditional."

Traditional folk songs are passed on to others by singing. Traditional folk music is learned by listening, not by reading the words or the musical notes.

Traditional folk music from the past and modern folk sounds of today are popular all over the world.

Musicians of all ages gathered for this folk song festival in eastern Kentucky.

SPREADING THE NEWS

In the past, especially in **rural** (RUR ul) areas, song was used as a way to spread the news. The words of a song worked much like a newspaper article would today—they spread the news to people in other towns.

What did people sing about? Some sang about a marriage or a new baby in the family. The story traveled by song, from town to town. Family and friends who lived in other towns soon heard the joyful news.

Many cultures around the world have used song to spread news from village to village.

THE BALLAD

A **ballad** (BAL ud) is a song that tells a story. Ballads are probably the best-known type of folk song. Ballads are short and simple. They usually name places, people, and dates. Ballads usually tell about one special event and get right to the point of the story.

A folk song that spreads the news of a new baby is a ballad. A folk song that tells of a sickness or death is also a ballad.

The guitar is a favorite instrument of many folksingers.

The clarinet is a variation of a folk reedpipe.

A xylophone is played by striking the bars with a light hammer.

THE EPIC

An **epic** (EP ik) is a long story or poem. An epic has a lot of details, unlike a ballad. A long folk song with many details is an epic folk song.

Epic folk songs often tell about an event like a battle or war. The event usually occurred a long time ago.

The main character in the song is generally a legend, or hero. The singer of the epic folk song tells how the hero suffered, and how the great deeds of the hero are admired by others.

Folk songs are a way to pass stories down from one generation to the next.

WORK SONGS

When you hear music, do you notice the beat? The beat is the the regular movement of sound.

Folk songs are sometimes sung to keep a beat. These kinds of folk songs are work songs. Railroad workers and farmhands sang work songs many years ago. The beat of the song helped them work at a regular pace.

Drums are used in ceremonies, to send messages and to create a musical sound.

FOLK MUSIC CHANGES

It isn't easy to learn a song just by hearing it sung, unless you hear it over and over. Try making up a simple song and sing it to a friend. Can your friend repeat it to another without making changes?

Since traditional folk songs are learned "by ear," the words and tunes easily change as the song is passed from singer to singer. The changes add personal style to the song.

A young musician plays an Autoharp.™

INSTRUMENTS

Voice can give music a special sound, but so do instruments. Each folk **culture** (KUL chur) can have their own common instruments.

The bagpipe is traditional in European folk music. The **dulcimer** (DUL suh mur) came from the Middle East. Drums and rattles are used in many cultures.

Popular instruments used in American folk music include the fiddle, banjo, guitar, mandolin, and flute.

Bagpipers play and march in a Saint Patrick's Day parade.

POPULAR FOLK TUNES

Folk music doesn't have to be passed on in the traditional way anymore. Radio, television, and the growing number of music stores make it easy for people to hear folk tunes.

Folk tunes like "Oh! Susanna" and "On Top of Old Smoky" are popular and familiar. Other folk songs may not be as familiar, but have sounds of other popular musical styles, like bluegrass, rock, and gospel.

GLOSSARY

ballad (BAL ud) — a simple song that tells a story

culture (KUL chur) — a society that has the same language, law, politics, religion, magic, art, and music

dulcimer (DUL suh mur) — a wire-stringed musical instrument that is either plucked, or struck with light hammers

epic (EP ik) — a long poem that tells of a hero's great deeds

rural (RUR ul) — country or farming area

tradition (truh DISH en) — the handing down of beliefs by telling or showing

INDEX

ballad   11, 14
epic   14
instruments
   bagpipe   20, 21
   banjo   20
   drum   5, 20
   dulcimer   20
   fiddle   20

flute   20
guitar   20
mandolin   20
rattles   20
xylophone   13
rural   9
tradition   6,
traditional   6, 19, 20, 22
work songs   16

FURTHER READING

Find out more about music with these helpful books and information sources:

• Forquer, Nancy E., and Marjorie Partin. *Music Bulletin Boards Activities Kit.*
   Parkers Publishing, 1990
• McLin, Lena. *Pulse: A History of Music.* Kjos West, 1977
• Nettl, Bruno. "Folk Music." Grolier Multimedia Encyclopedia, 1998
• Nettl, Bruno. "Folk Music." Microsoft Encarta Encyclopedia, 1996